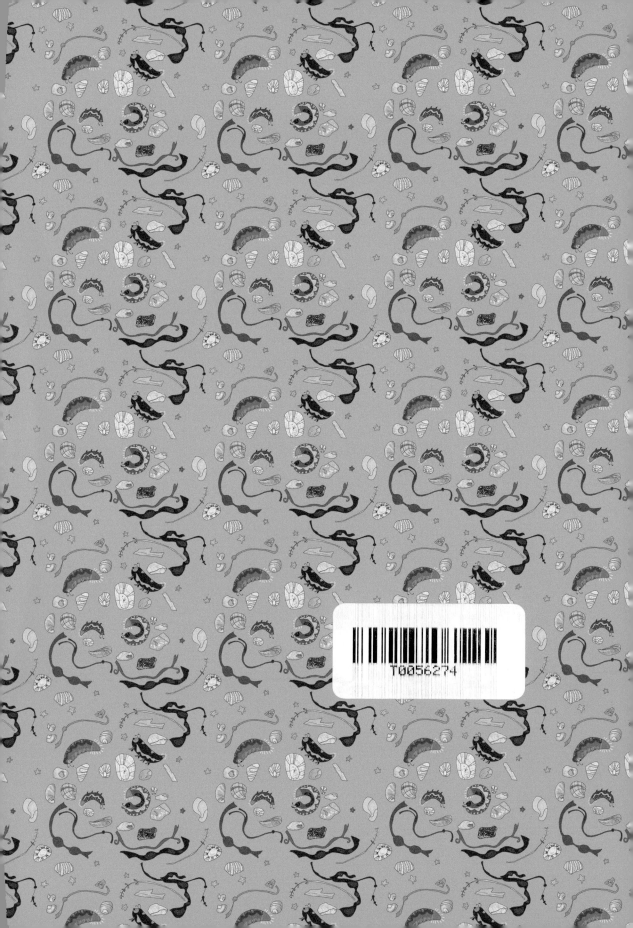

T0056274

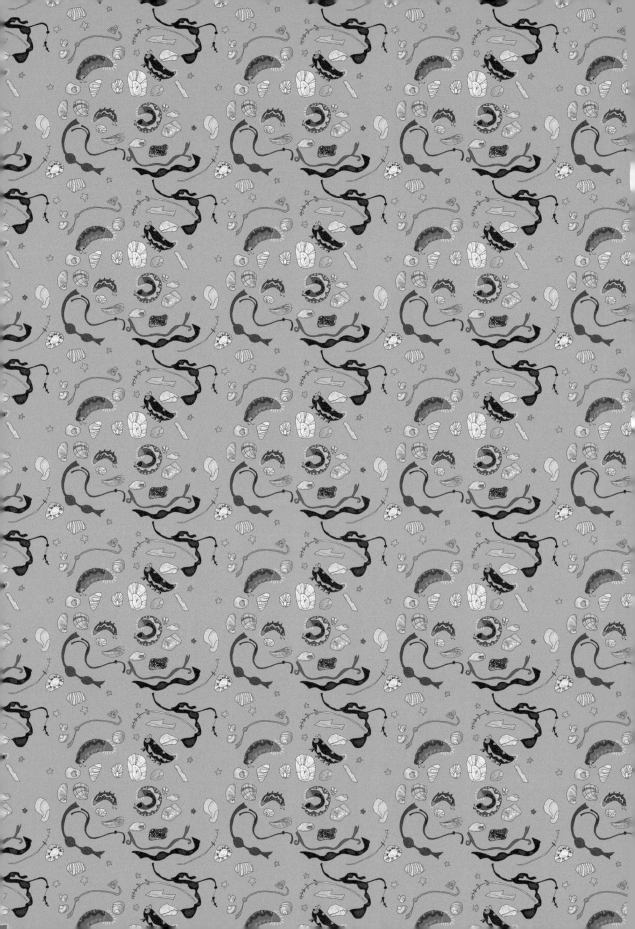

Zedie

Zoola

Zeel

Mishposh

Tibul

Demshoo

Miply

Wonpeel

Limtop

Alya

Pibbon

Hishkit

Nipteef

Glorm

Zeel with the Alans

ZigZag Cove

Kippo

Access your online resources

Zedie & Zoola's Playful Universe is accompanied by a number of printable online materials designed to ensure this resource best supports your professional needs.

Activate your online resources:

Go to www.routledge.com/cw/speechmark and click on the cover of this book.

Click the 'Sign in or Request Access' button and follow the instructions in order to access the resources.

Zedie & Zoola's Playful Universe

Playtime is essential for children's wellbeing and provides key opportunities to make friends. Yet for some children, unstructured play can present real challenges.

This beautifully illustrated guide is designed to be used alongside:

- **Zedie & Zoola's Playtime Cards** – a pack of 25 cards containing ideas for fun playground games that draw from *Zedie & Zoola's Playful Universe* and encourage children with different communication styles to play together.

- **Zedie & Zoola Light Up the Night** – a colourful storybook, which draws on themes relating to friendships, neurodiversity, participation, and advocacy.

The cards and storybook explore the topic of communication differences through engaging characters and games. This accompanying guide offers additional advice for adults to use the cards effectively, with helpful contextual information to assist in making playtimes more accessible for children with communication conditions.

This is an essential resource for parents, primary school teachers, and speech and language therapists, as well as anyone looking for new ways to foster an inclusive environment to help children aged 6-9 with different communication styles engage and play with their peers.

Vanessa Lloyd-Esenkaya holds a PhD in child psychology. Her research explores the social side of Developmental Language Disorder (DLD) and is published in scientific journals. She is currently training to be a speech and language therapist and lives in Kent with her family.

ZEdiE & ZooLA'S PLAYFUL UNIVERSE

A Practical Guide to Supporting Children with Different Communication Styles at Playtime

Written and illustrated by

Vanessa Lloyd-Esenkaya

Cover image: Vanessa Lloyd-Esenkaya

First published 2023
by Routledge
4 Park Square, Milton Park, Abingdon, Oxon OX14 4RN

and by Routledge
605 Third Avenue, New York, NY 10158

Routledge is an imprint of the Taylor & Francis Group, an informa business

British Library Cataloguing-in-Publication Data
A catalogue record for this book is available from the British Library

Library of Congress Cataloging-in-Publication Data
Names: Lloyd-Esenkaya, Vanessa, author.
Title: Zedie and Zoola's playful universe: a practical guide to supporting children with different communication styles at playtime/Vanessa Lloyd-Esenkaya.
Description: Abingdon, Oxon; New York, NY: Routledge, 2023. | Includes bibliographical references and index. |
Identifiers: LCCN 2022022163 (print) | LCCN 2022022164 (ebook) | ISBN 9780367651183 (paperback) | ISBN 9781003332473 (ebook)
Subjects: LCSH: Play–Social aspects. | Play–Psychological aspects. | Early childhood education–Activity programs. | Communicative disorders in children. | Inclusive education.
Classification: LCC LB1139.35.P55 L556 2023 (print) | LCC LB1139.35.P55 (ebook) |
DDC 155.4/18–dc23/eng/20220825
LC record available at https://lccn.loc.gov/2022022163
LC ebook record available at https://lccn.loc.gov/2022022164

ISBN: 9780367651183 (pbk)
ISBN: 9781003332473 (ebk)

DOI: 10.4324/9781003332473

Typeset in VAGRounded or Calibri or Antitled
by Deanta Global Publishing Services, Chennai, India

Printed in the UK by Severn, Gloucester on responsibly sourced paper

Access the companion website: www.routledge.com/cw/speechmark

For my family, and all the kids who've taught me.

Zedie & Zoola's Playful Universe

Guidebook

This book provides a guide to communication differences and children's play. The playing cards, storybook, and online resources which accompany this book are tools which children can use to participate in playtime activities.

Children's storybook

Zedie & Zoola Light Up the Night is a beautifully illustrated story which draws on themes relating to friendships, neurodiversity, participation, and advocacy.

Pack of 25 playtime game cards

PLAY!

Age 6+

Premium online content

- Playing card duplicates
- Log-book
- Colouring sheets
- Wall poster
- Sign board for the playground
- Play access cards
- Lesson plan and presentation
- Sign-out form

Acknowledgements

It was such a simple idea that I wondered why we hadn't thought of it before. When I worked as a learning support assistant in a primary school, my colleagues and I were unsure how to involve all the children in playground activities. There was one child who was desperate to join in but spent most lunchtimes on the fringes of the playground hubbub. One day, a speech and language therapist (SLT) suggested that we give her a real object, show her how to play, and show her how to ask her friends to play. That was when we realised that the games her friends were playing were so fast-paced and abstract that it was hard for her to find a foothold. We discovered that ordinary objects, like bouncy balls, could become tools to unlock barriers to play.

My central aim in creating *Zedie & Zoola's Playful Universe* has been to make playtimes accessible to all children. Throughout the entire process of making this resource, I have been informed by the social model of disability, which focuses on the environment as being disabling, and the emerging neurodiversity movement, which considers the uniqueness of every human being to be a natural part of life.

One of the hardest parts of writing the guidebook for *Zedie & Zoola's Playful Universe* has been finding the right language to describe different communication styles. I have used identity-first language to talk about autism (e.g. "autistic people") instead of person-first language (e.g. "people with autism") because accumulating research shows that viewing autism as an intrinsic part of one's identity is the overwhelming preference of many autistic people. I have also intentionally used neutral language to describe the features of different communication "conditions". It has been difficult to select an appropriate term to talk about distinct styles of communicating which are given a diagnostic label. After much deliberation, I settled on the word "condition" which I define as *a state of being*. While this is the best term that I can think of, it is still not perfect. The language around neurodiversity and the language that SLTs/Developmental Psychologists use to define communication differences is still developing, and I would hope that my own thoughts and the language that I use will continue to be challenged, to change, and to grow over the coming years.

Zedie & Zoola's Playful Universe is an extension of the work I started during my PhD, and I am grateful to my brilliant PhD supervisors who guided me throughout my doctoral research journey. As part of my PhD, I invented a cartoon character. I made a series of animations about the cartoon character for the purpose of creating a new research tool. The character stayed with me, and when I started to imagine where they might live, I pictured ZigZag Cove and all the personalities who live there.

The key acknowledgement I want to make relates to the voices who have shaped Chapter 2 of the guidebook. I have drawn from many first-person accounts to write about the experience of stammering and of Developmental Language Disorder (DLD). There are many brilliant advocates who have powerfully shared their lived experiences of stammering and of DLD through videos, podcasts, and blogs, and the summaries I have written are an amalgamation of these. I have drawn most of my inspiration from the first-hand accounts compiled by Stamma and Raising Awareness of Developmental Language Disorder (RADLD). Both organisations are important for educating the public on what it's really like to stammer or to have DLD. Where I have taken inspiration from a specific comment that an advocate has made, I have cited them in the text. My own interactions with young people who have DLD, and my interactions with their families, have also informed this chapter. As an adult without a communication condition, I will never truly know what it is like to have any of the distinct communication styles that I have described in this guidebook. I hope that by drawing widely from different first-hand accounts I have been able to go some way to overcome this barrier.

I am grateful to my whole family for helping me to turn my ideas into something real. Thanks goes to dad, for encouraging me to write, mum, for encouraging me to draw, and Adam, for being there when I needed you. Thank you so much to Jasmine, Scarlett, and Joseph for being excellent game-testers! Thank you for trying out the games and for giving such helpful and supportive feedback (thank you John, Mandy, and Zoe too!). Nicky, thank you for cheerleading me on whenever I sent you a new character or painting to look at. Bora and Lydia, I'm really grateful to both of you for looking over my drafts and giving your honest opinions! Tayfun, you're the best. Thank you for embracing all our new, colourful friends, and for allowing me to live as much in ZigZag Cove as in the real world for the last two years. I'm so lucky to have you and I feel really grateful that you've let me share every single tiny idea and worry with you. Thanks for all the ingenious ideas from your brain! Lastly, my enormous thanks goes to Clare and the rest of the Routledge team for believing in me.

Contents

DOI: 10.4324/9781003332473-1

Background to neurodiversity

One of the most wonderful truths that we can rely on in the natural world is that variation is everywhere. Two leaves from an oak tree might look the same from a distance, but study up close and you will see their shapes differ slightly and one has more veins than the other. Every crystal is unique. No two butterfly wings carry the same constellation of scales. The same natural variation is true of people. Each one of us carries an infinite web of experiences, skills, preferences, and fears. The ways that we perceive situations, plan our behaviour, and reflect on our actions differs from person to person. It is inevitable that no two minds are the same. We can call this natural variation among all human minds *neurodiversity*.

One of the skills that humans do particularly well with is to categorise information. We do it all the time. "Look, a dog!" the toddler says, pointing to a lion at the zoo. Well, it might have four legs but it's certainly not a dog. Animal families, species, we constantly organise our world like clean clothes in wardrobes. Each concept gets its own name and place in the system. Categories are useful because they help us to make sense of the world around us.

Today, whole textbooks can be found which categorise the human experience. Sometimes characteristic ways of thinking, experiences, or behaviours cluster together enough to be categorised as distinct ways of being. This is the case with neurodevelopmental conditions,[1] such as autism, Attention Deficit Hyperactivity Disorder (ADHD), and dyslexia. No two autistic people are the same (of course!) but an autistic person is likely to find someone with similar experiences to theirs within a community of people who share the same type of neurodivergence. Some styles of communicating can be identified as distinct communication conditions, such as situational mutism or Speech Sound Disorder (SSD). Categorising human beings in this way can help us to make sense of our identity and our experiences.

Returning to the natural variation among all human minds, it is natural and expected that we all have different ways of thinking, and different ways of interacting with our world and one another. Human societies benefit from the presence of varied perspectives. New ideas based on diverse experiences can help us to find effective solutions to problems. The unique perspective that we each bring to a team is something to value.

To celebrate the natural diversity among all of us, we should create habitats (places, services, organisations) which welcome everyone. We have a habit of designing environments with our eyes fixed solely on the ways that *most* people engage with the world. This is the easiest way, but it is also excluding for many people. Playgrounds are generally designed for children who experience no barriers to communication. Children are left to their own devices to fill an expanse of concrete or grass with simply their imaginations and voices. It can be hard for some children to integrate into these environments, where fast-paced verbal interactions are highly prized. We can strive to adapt our environments to welcome the 10 per cent of children who have speech, language, and communication needs[1] into the community.

For a truly inclusive society, we all need:

1. **Understanding:** Know that all of us are unique. No two minds are the same.
2. **Acceptance:** We are all different and that's expected. We take one another as we are.
3. **Openness to grow:** When we notice someone being excluded, we ask ourselves what we can do to make it easier for them to participate.
4. **Celebration:** We see our uniqueness as a gift. We value the diversity we create.

Zedie & Zoola's Playful Universe is guided by these four principles.

Note

1 *Condition* NOUN
   Definition: a state of being

DOI: 10.4324/9781003332473-2

Communication differences

Communication underpins every aspect of our lives. We use it to tell stories, to share secrets, and to make people laugh. It is the medium through which all our education is taught. It helps us to find out about other people's personalities, what they like and dislike, whether we hold the same opinions, and whether they are the sort of person we want to know more about. We use it to share our deepest thoughts and our most basic needs. Communication is a fundamental human right.

Communication needs are one of the most common forms of childhood disability. Communication needs are very variable and encompass a wide range of characteristics including, but not limited to, participation barriers to:

- understanding what others are saying through speech/sign language/written information;

- putting words in order when speaking/signing/writing;

- forming sounds;

- making speech come out fluently;

- understanding what others mean or how they are feeling from their behaviour, facial expressions, tone of voice, or the intonation or stress they put on words.

Despite being something that we use all the time, we tend not to give a lot of thought to communication. When we really think about it, what is communication? What is language? Perhaps a mini dictionary will be useful here:

Communication	The process of sharing information. It can take many forms: speaking, listening, gesturing, and use of pictures, to name a few.
Language	Where a system of communication, including speaking, writing, or signing (e.g. British Sign Language), is used to convey meaning.
Speech	One vehicle for carrying language.
Voice	The sound escaping the lips. It is created by the orchestra that is the lungs, throat, and mouth.

Communication conditions seen in children

Communication is a broad concept. We share information in most aspects of our lives, and this information-sharing takes many forms. We can find different styles of communication, which are categorised as distinct communication conditions, in many different areas. The term 'condition' describes a state of being. Some communication conditions affect language, some affect speech, others affect the social use of communication. Some conditions affect involuntary sounds and movements, and others affect the voice. Figure 1 gives a non-exhaustive overview of some of the communication conditions seen in children. Many of these are not specific to childhood, adults can have the same conditions. We can experience more than one of these conditions at the same time. Sometimes children's communication styles do not quite fit the criteria for the categories drawn in Figure 1, but they might still benefit from extra communication tools to participate in everyday activities.

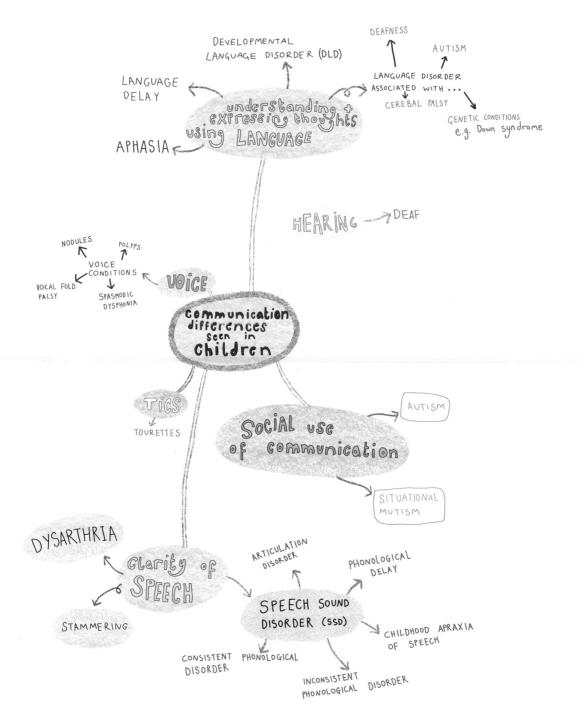

Figure 1 An overview of some of the communication conditions seen in children.

Causes of communication variability

There are all sorts of variations in our biology, our habitats, and the events we live through, which create the natural variation we find in our communication styles. The science of communication is a mammoth subject and there's plenty to learn about. Let's take a look at the different circumstances that can cause some of the communication conditions we see in children. We'll see how biology, chemistry, genetics, and different situations, like injury and infections, can affect the ways we communicate.

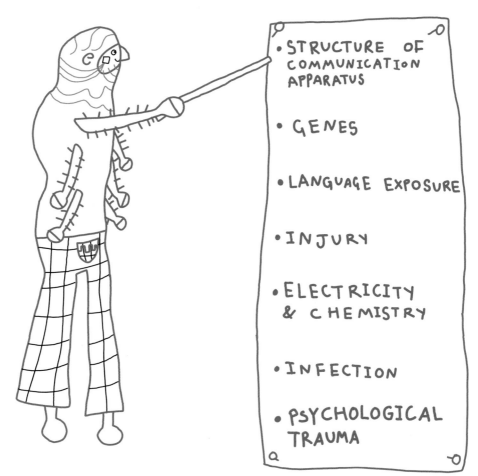

- STRUCTURE OF COMMUNICATION APPARATUS
- GENES
- LANGUAGE EXPOSURE
- INJURY
- ELECTRICITY & CHEMISTRY
- INFECTION
- PSYCHOLOGICAL TRAUMA

Structure of communication apparatus

Our natural body structures can affect the ways we communicate. Some of us are born with a cleft lip and palate. Our palate is the roof of our mouth. A cleft describes a gap or split. We can have a cleft lip and palate when parts of our face do not fuse together while we are developing in the womb. Many of us will have surgery in early life to close the gaps between the parts of our face that have not fused. It is common for our speech and/or language to be affected for multiple reasons. The way our face is structured can affect the way that we form sounds when we speak.[2] When we have a gap in our lip or the roof of our mouth, we might make speech sounds in a different way to most people, so other people might not understand some of what we say. Also, when we are born with a cleft lip and/or palate, we have a higher chance of having glue ear (temporary hearing loss caused by a build-up of fluid in our ear canal), which can affect our language development. Therefore, when we are young, we might have a language delay.[3,4]

Genes

Sometimes small variations in our genes create constellations of characteristics where our communication style is affected. For example, when we have an extra chromosome (a structure which holds a group of genes) we can have Down syndrome. Language, speech, and the social use of communication can be affected when we have Down syndrome, as well as our memory and learning.[5] Also, when we have Down syndrome, our genetic makeup can increase our susceptibility to ear infections, which sometimes affect our hearing.[6] Other types of neurodivergence created by our gene patterns, which can influence our communication style, include Fragile X syndrome, Williams syndrome, Kabuki syndrome, Klinefelter syndrome, Triple X syndrome, and Unique Rare Chromosome Disorders.[7]

Some of us have a type of neurodivergence where the exact cause is unknown but there is evidence for a genetic basis. For example, autism is thought to have a genetic basis.[8] Autism affects the social use of communication. Those of us who are autistic often take language literally, even when people are using figures of speech like "can you give me a hand?" or are being sarcastic. We can have trouble understanding non-autistic people and they can have trouble understanding us.[9] Some of us find it hard to find the words we want to say.[10] Some of us use little or no verbal communication and use alternatives to speech to communicate.[11]

Language exposure

There is wide variation in the pace that we each develop language in early childhood. Around 7–14 per cent of us begin primary school with 'weak' language skills.[12] This figure could be higher for those who started school in 2020, in the midst of the Covid-19 pandemic. During this time, children were unable to play with each other and parents had to juggle careers and caring responsibilities in extraordinary and stressful circumstances. A 2021 report in England found 96 per cent of schools surveyed were concerned about the communication skills of the 4–5 year olds who started school during the pandemic, believing more of these children needed support for their language skills than previous year groups.[13] More children than usual might have experienced a language delay during the pandemic because of reduced exposure to language in the environment.[14–16] When we have a language delay, early interventions which focus on our listening and narrative skills, building our vocabulary, and our ability to recognise the sounds that make up words, can help us to catch up.[17]

Injury

If a strong force hits our heads, for example if we knock our head during a car accident, our brain can be injured, which can affect our communication skills. A Traumatic Brain Injury (TBI), which includes concussion, can affect our speech, language, and social use of communication.[18, 19] It might also affect our hearing, and our attention, memory, and learning.[20, 21]

Electricity and chemistry

Some of us experience epilepsy as children. This happens when we have seizures. Seizures are bursts of electrical activity in the brain. When we have epilepsy, our speech and social use of communication can be affected.[22, 23] The seizures might also cause us to develop a language disorder called aphasia.[24] Aphasia is where we lose some of the language skills we used to have. We might have trouble understanding what others mean when they talk, and we might find it hard to express ourselves when we talk.

Our brains need a regular supply of blood to function because our blood carries vital chemical compounds. Some of us experience a stroke during childhood. A stroke happens when the blood flow to our brain stops or weakens, causing our brain cells to start dying. This can change the ways that parts of our brain operate.

We might lose our ability to speak, and we might lose our understanding of language.[25] Our social use of communication can also be affected, as well as our attention and learning.[26, 27] When we have a stroke in childhood, we might be able to relearn many of the skills we had before, but our path of development could be altered.[28] We might have a new style of communicating after the stroke and we might ask for tools to participate in activities many years later.[29]

Infection

Different infections in our body can change the ways our communication apparatus operates. Meningitis is one infection that can affect our communication. Meningitis infects the protective membranes which wrap around our brain and spinal cord, which can change the way our brain functions. Meningitis can affect our speech, language, and social use of communication.[30] Meningitis might also affect our hearing, and our attention, memory, and learning.[31, 32]

Psychological trauma

Experiencing trauma in childhood can have a significant impact on us. The development of post-traumatic stress disorder (PTSD) during childhood can affect the ways we process information and it can affect our memory and learning.[33] The experience of trauma might also create communication differences for some of us. Those of us who are exposed to trauma as children, such as abuse, neglect, natural disasters, or war, are more likely to have weaker language skills than those who have not been exposed to trauma.[33–36] This is a relatively young field of research and we still need more studies to learn whether childhood psychological trauma has a direct impact on language development.

Understanding and celebrating diverse communication styles

We will now have a closer look at two communication conditions. This will help us to picture the impact that a communication condition can have on our everyday lives. It will also (hopefully!) give us a chance to reflect on the ways that we can make our environments more inclusive. We'll start with a style of communication that most of us are vaguely familiar with: Stammering. Then we'll focus on the most common communication condition, which you may know little about[37]: Developmental Language Disorder (DLD).

Stammering

Stammering, also known as stuttering, is a type of neurodivergence affecting speech. Stammering includes repeating sounds involuntarily, making words longer, or being unable to get words out. When we have a stammer, there are likely to be certain situations where we know we are going to stammer. For example, when we're expected to introduce ourselves, we might know that we're likely to stammer saying our name. There might be certain words or sounds which we know we stammer more on too. On rare occasions an injury, such as a force to the head or a brain tumour, can cause us to stammer.[18] More often, a stammer is something we happen to grow up with.[38] The technical term for this is developmental stammering.

It is not known what causes developmental stammering to happen, but it probably results from the natural variation in the ways our different brains develop and operate.

What does our communication look like?

- **It takes a while to explain what we mean.**
  When we repeat sounds or we have difficulty getting words out, it can take a while for us to say what we want to say.

- **Other people try to finish our sentences.**
  When our stammer makes us take a long time to speak, other people often try to complete our sentences for us. This can be very frustrating! Sometimes people guess wrong what we are trying to say. Other times, people guess correctly, and it can feel like a relief at first to have someone fill in our sentence but afterwards it can make us feel ashamed of our stammer.[39] It's better when people accept our stammer and give us time to speak.

- **Our conversation flows easily.**
  When we have a stammer, we are unlikely to experience difficulties or reveal our difficulties with speaking all the time. When we feel relaxed, we might stammer less. Sometimes we can use strategies to reduce our stammer, for example we might have breathing techniques, or ways to suppress certain words, which help us to speak without stammering. Some of these techniques can take a lot of effort. Just because our stammer is reduced does not mean it has disappeared.

- **We appear shy or uncomfortable in social situations.**
  When a stammer makes talking difficult, we might avoid talking altogether. We might avoid eye contact or avoid introducing ourselves to get out of situations that require us to speak. It's stressful when people put us on the spot to speak, for example when we are asked to give presentations, so we might avoid situations which put us in this situation. When we accept our stammer and feel less anxious about being judged by others, we can feel more confident to be ourselves.

- **We seem to be nervous or indecisive.**
  When we stammer, it might seem like we are frightened and anxious to voice our opinions, or that we are unsure of what to say. This is a misconception. We know exactly what we want to say, we are simply unable to make our words come out fluently all the time.[39]

- **Other people lose their patience with us.**
  When our stammer makes us take a longer time to say what we want to say, others can stop listening, or worse, tell us to hurry up! When others put pressure on us to speed up our talking, our stammer is likely to increase in intensity, making it even harder for us to speak.[39] This can make us feel intensely embarrassed and upset and it can have a lasting impact on our mental health.

Celebrating us

Diversity in the ways that we all speak is natural and expected, and nobody should be made to feel ashamed for stammering. There are ways to adapt environments to make situations more accessible for those of us who stammer to participate, and to help us feel more comfortable:

- **Time:** When we are having a conversation, allow us plenty of time to say what we are trying to say. A conversation involves both of us and there is no need for us to rush.

- **Give options:** If there are activities which usually require speaking (e.g. drama clubs, presentations, reading aloud), create ways for people to participate which do not require speaking. We might not be able to join in by speaking today, but we don't want to miss out altogether.

- **Kindness and respect:** There are no right or wrong ways of speaking. If it is noticeable that we are having difficulties in making our words come out, there is no need for anyone else to feel embarrassed by this. Being treated with dignity helps us to accept and feel proud of our differences.

Developmental Language Disorder

Developmental Language Disorder (DLD) is a type of neurodivergence affecting language. It includes difficulties with understanding what others are saying, learning new vocabulary, and expressing our thoughts in our native language.[40] It is something we are born with and continues into adulthood. When we speak more than one language, DLD affects each of the languages we speak.[1] Did you know that 2 in 30 of us have DLD?[41] This can be a very hidden condition. Some of us have DLD without knowing it. If we have DLD, we might develop strategies to cope with the challenges we encounter, which can incidentally stop others from realising we have any difficulties with language. It is not known what causes DLD, but it might have a genetic basis.[42] It's possible that genetic variations might affect the ways our brains spot the patterns that make up the hidden rules of language.[43, 44]

How to spot DLD in the classroom

If you are a teacher or teaching assistant, you may have children in your school who have DLD, and nobody knows it. When children's communication challenges are recognised, support can be put in place to make sure they are thriving in school, not just surviving. A speech and language therapist is qualified to formally identify DLD. The following characteristics can be indicators of a hidden language disorder:

- **A child who is struggling with their schoolwork.**
  Language is a tool for learning. Many activities, including reading, writing, and maths, are made harder when people have DLD. Lots of people with DLD also have dyslexia (reading, writing, and spelling difficulties) and even those without dyslexia can find reading and writing difficult due to comprehension challenges.

- **A child who is restless.**
  Children with DLD must work hard to maintain focus during lessons and during conversations. DLD makes it difficult to understand language which means school can be tiring. Also, lots of people with DLD also have Attention Deficit Hyperactivity Disorder (ADHD).

- **A child who waits for others to respond before following instructions.**
  DLD can make it hard to follow verbal instructions. To cope with this, children with DLD often watch to see what others do when instructions are given, to know what to do next.

- **A child who is having friendship challenges.**
  Challenges with understanding language or expressing oneself verbally can make it harder for children to integrate into peer groups, participate in games on the playground, express how they are feeling, and resolve arguments. Unfortunately, children with DLD are vulnerable to bullying.

What does our communication look like?

- **Other people think we are not listening to what they are saying.**
  DLD can make it hard for us to process everything someone says, particularly if they are speaking quickly. It feels like people's words are escaping their mouths too quickly for us to keep up.[45] It is disheartening when other people think we are not listening, not paying attention, or not intelligent. In fact, we are highly capable, but language can be a barrier to our understanding. We might need someone to repeat what they have said, or to say it in another way.

- **Others get confused by what we are saying.**
  DLD can make it hard to learn the hidden rules of language, so we might use different words from those we really mean. For example, we might say "I am moved the chair", when we really mean "I am moving the chair", or "he" when we really mean "she". The person we're speaking to might not understand what we are trying to say straight away.

- **Other people lose their patience with us.**
  When we have DLD it can be hard to think of the words we want to say, and to make sentences which other people will understand. Expressing ourselves can be difficult and we very frequently experience the feeling that a word is on the tip of our tongue, but we can't get it out. Sometimes, when our DLD makes us take a long time to speak, other people get frustrated with us and become impatient. This can be embarrassing and stressful. It's better when we have enough processing time during conversations to express ourselves.

- **We appear shy or uncomfortable in social situations.**
  When DLD makes it hard for us to understand what others are saying, or to express ourselves verbally, socialising can throw us obstacles. We might prefer to watch other people socialising than to participate ourselves, even if we would like to be able to join in. We might be very quiet in group situations because we are concentrating so much on following the conversation.[46] It can be hard to explain to other people what DLD is and to make it known when we're struggling. When our friends understand and accept our differences, and know how to support us, we can feel more confident to be ourselves.[47]

- **Our conversation flows easily.**
  DLD affects us differently. Some of us are very talkative; we love chatting to people, making new friends, and joining in with conversations. However, even when we are very chatty, we might still find it hard to understand what people say to us, and we could have trouble expressing our feelings or remembering the words we want to say. Our difficulties with language are often invisible.

Celebrating us

When we have DLD, we bring a diverse set of experiences to the table, and we should be proud of our identity. There are ways that we can make environments accessible to those of us who have DLD, so that everyone can participate:

- **Patience:** When we are having a conversation, give us time to process what's been said. Say things in a different way if we haven't understood the first time. Give us time to express what we mean so that we can be understood.

- **Visuals:** Not knowing what's coming next or what we've been asked to do is stressful. When creating environments such as schools, communicate information in a visual way. Verbal information disappears and can be forgotten, whereas written information and images are permanent.

- **Advocacy:** Asking for help is a valuable skill for everyone to learn. Create environments where we feel confident to ask for help when we need support. Finding ways to tell other people what we find challenging and what helps to make things easier is empowering and helps us to become independent.

Many of the ways we can make environments more inclusive for those who stammer and those who have DLD could translate to other communication conditions and could even be useful for those without a communication condition. Visual information, for example, can be helpful for everyone.

All of us deserve to be treated with respect, dignity, and kindness. Since all of us are different, and nobody else can know our experiences as well as we do, the best way that others can find out how to support us is to ask us what we would find helpful. Our priorities might look very different to the goals that other people have for us.[48] Other people may not be aware that there are certain things that we would like to be able to do but feel we can't because of barriers in our way. When it comes to children, and the school environment, speech and language therapists, occupational therapists, clinical psychologists, and educational psychologists are useful people for teachers and parents to gain advice from, about how to ask children what they would like support with, and about ways to adapt the environment to enable participation.

Note

1 An important note on multilingualism: Exposure to more than one language does not cause DLD.[68] When we have DLD or other communication conditions we can learn more than one language. Exposure to multiple languages in our early life will not confuse us or negatively impact our language development.[69] In fact, the ability to access more than one language could enhance our communication opportunities.[69] Exposure to multiple languages is a precious gift with many advantages, not least strengthening our relationships with people and cultures.[70]

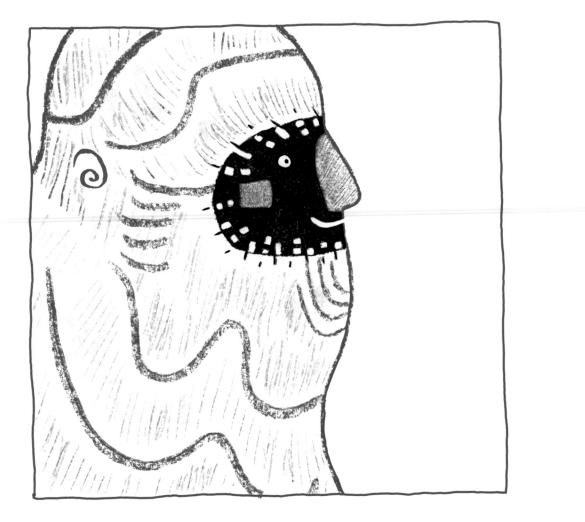

DOI: 10.4324/9781003332473-3

Magic on the playground

As children, we fill our worlds with excitement, risk, and imagination. We spend hours inventing stories, giving ourselves new roles to try out, new shoes to wear, new voices to try for size. We pretend to argue, and we really do argue when something isn't fair. We run, skip, and hide with a seemingly endless energy. So, what were we thinking about back in those days? And what was the point of it all, was there a purpose?

These questions have challenged researchers for decades, and their answers have had important consequences for the lives of children. Today, play is thought to be so essential that it is enshrined within the United Nations Declaration of Human Rights. While delegates from all corners of the world decided that every one of us is born equal in dignity and rights, they agreed that every child has the fundamental right to "relax and play" and to "freedom of expression", which all parties surrounding a child must respect and promote.[49]

To understand the impact that play has on human development, it's useful to know about the different ways that children play. To make sense of the tangled webs of laughter and chaos in the playground, we can categorise play into different subtypes[50, 51]:

Type of play	Description
Exploration (object play, exploratory play, and creative play)	Being curious about objects and investigating physical aspects of the environment with our senses. Could involve making things out of materials and getting messy.
Symbolic play	Using objects or signs to represent something else, for example using a stick for a key.
Mastery play	Shaping the environment around us, for example digging holes in the soil, or building dens.
Physical activity play/locomotor play	Movement activities, such as running, jumping, balancing, skipping with ropes, and dancing.
Playground games with rules	Games involving rules that we make up ourselves, or that have been passed down to us, such as "Duck, Duck, Goose", and "Cops and Robbers".
Play fighting/ rough-and-tumble play	Physical contact through wrestling, pushing, hitting, or tickling, for the sake of fun on both sides.
Sports and fitness	Ball games and athletics such as football, volleyball, and swimming.
Deep play/risky play	Playing with a risk of negative consequences such as accidents or embarrassment, e.g., climbing trees, and 'truth or dare'.
Communication play	Playing through using words (for example by telling jokes), body language, and through using our facial expressions to have fun.
Clapping games and rhyming songs	Clapping games that we make up ourselves, or that have been passed down to us, and might be accompanied by songs, e.g. "A Sailor Went to Sea, Sea, Sea".
Acting out (role play, imaginative play, dramatic play, sociodramatic play)	Acting out scenes based on our own reality, based on the roles we see other people perform (such as a baby, or a bus driver), or based on something unreal (such as a unicorn). Might involve physical props and costumes, or the props could be entirely imagined.

Some of these subtypes of play are seen at earlier ages than others. For example, a one-year-old might pick up plastic animals in a sandpit, stroke them, and have a go at putting the head of one into her mouth (i.e. exploratory play), but she hasn't yet developed the cognitive skills to pretend to be a dinosaur while her brother is a tiger and together they need to save the world from the ocean monsters (i.e. imaginative play). There is no "right" way to play at any age. As children, we all have our own preferences for the types of play we most enjoy, and who we most like to play with.

Why play is important?

When we play, we are mentally engaged and often physically active. Play is shown to be linked to better physical health outcomes and better emotional wellbeing.[52,53] It can help us to gain a feeling of stability and belonging because it lets us express our emotions and fears in a safe environment, and it gives us a way to bond with the people around us. [54, 55] There are so many skills that might be developed during play that we can organise them into the following categories:

Opportunities that play provides	Skills/attributes that could be developed
Learn about the body, and what it can/cannot do.	Motor skills.
Learn about the surrounding environment and how things work.	Problem-solving and analytical skills.
Ability to take risks: overcome fear of physical injury or social risks.	Ability to manage future threats.
Learn about real life social situations, and how to handle them.	Problem-solving skills. Communication and social skills. Ability to cope with future adversity.
Develop understanding of own and others' emotions.	Emotional and social skills.
Establish and maintain friendships.	Social skills and support emotional wellbeing.
Learn to tell stories and develop characters for difference roles.	Narrative skills and creativity. Self-expression skills to support self-esteem and wellbeing.

Of course, we don't really think about any of these things when we're playing. We just do it because it's fun. It makes us feel free and relaxed. Researchers have asked children, the real experts, what they think about playing. Some of their responses were[56, 57]:

- "It feels like you're really happy and you're like you don't want it to stop".

- "Play is a kind of rest. If you continue doing something without rest, you will do it worse and worse".

- "I feel very unhappy if I can't play. It feels like there's something always making me very angry".

- "I probably wouldn't learn anything if I didn't have time to play. I [would] probably just be really bored".

So as children, we play because it feels good, and when we don't play, we feel bad, distressed, and possibly even angry. While play is undeniably fun, it is also essential for children's wellbeing. We must respect and protect it and make space for all children out there on the playground.

The language of play

Communication is a key ingredient to life on the playground. Picture a school field in the summertime with a hundred children roaming about. Some kids are scoring goals on the football pitch, some are searching for ladybirds in the newly cut grass, and some are chasing one another while shouting names. When all of this is going on, communication is used to ask to join games and to learn the rules once we've entered. When a game of make-believe is happening, we use communication to create stories and new identities. When we wrestle someone to the ground, communication is needed to signal the difference between enjoyment and real distress. When arguments take place, we use communication to diffuse tensions and find solutions.

Many children with communication conditions find some aspects of playtimes hard to navigate. Take these examples:

- **Situational mutism –** Research finds children with situational mutism (also called selective mutism), who rarely speak at school and often experience social anxiety, have greater difficulties making friends than children without situational mutism.[58]

- **Speech conditions (e.g. Speech Sound Disorder) –** Siblings of children with speech conditions have described the ways they protect their brother/sister from being misunderstood or teased by other children by acting as a translator and by speaking on their behalf.[59]

- **Developmental Language Disorder (DLD) –** Children with DLD often have difficulties accessing play, understanding others' intentions, and resolving conflicts, and are vulnerable to bullying.[60, 61] Parents often work hard to make their children's teachers, friends, and friends' parents understand DLD, to prevent their child from being socially excluded.[62]

When we face barriers to playing with others and making friends as children, there can be long-term effects. As a teenager with DLD, we are more likely to have a low state of mental health if we had friendship difficulties during childhood.[63] Similarly, as an adult who stammers, we are more likely to experience social anxiety and depression if we were bullied as a child.[64]

Magic on the playground

All of us are different. Some children with communication conditions have no need for support on the playground. They enjoy playtimes and have friends who know them well. Other children with communication conditions do find it hard to participate at playtime, and this puts their future health and wellbeing at risk. We should make space for everyone on the playground and that means adapting playtimes to make them accessible to all styles of communication. This ambition lies at the heart of *Zedie & Zoola's Playful Universe*.

Increasing participation at playtime

Researchers have begun to study the links between communication conditions and children's social interactions at playtime, but there is still a great deal to learn.[60] New insights into the most effective ways to support children at playtime are likely to reveal themselves in the future. For now, the following ideas may help to make school playtimes more inclusive:

Suggested ways to make school playtimes more inclusive for all communication styles	
Create quiet spaces	Reducing background noise can help children with hearing, speech, or language conditions to communicate.
Provide clear and concise information on signs	If spaces in the playground are designed for a specific purpose, or there are playground rules for all to follow, use signs to make this information visible and accessible to all. Use communication boards in the playground (see our online content!) for children to point to as an alternative to verbal communication.
Alternative options at playtime: indoor activities, structured games	Some children may prefer activities such as board games, music groups, colouring, or adult-led playground games, over free-play. Provide options to suit different children's preferences, needs, and capabilities.
Provide props to play with, beyond early years settings: scrap materials, hoops, chalk, whiteboards, and pens	The presence of objects can provide a starting point for play, meaning children do not need to rely solely on their imagination and verbal skills.
Incentives to reduce social isolation	Reward children who have been observed making accommodations for others to join them in play. Also praise children who self-advocate to make their needs known, while respecting any preferences that children have for not feeling singled out.[65]
Trusted members of staff	Make children aware of a member of staff they can turn to if they have worries or need support for their friendships. School staff should look out for children with communication conditions, who are vulnerable to bullying.[64, 66, 67]
Time and visuals to support in managing emotions, problem solving, and resolving conflicts	Playtime provides opportunities for children to learn important social skills. Create time in the school day for children to process social situations, such as causes and consequences of playtime conflicts. Use visuals to aid children's understanding.
Support to learn how to access and initiate play independently	When supervising playtimes, step in to support children who want to socialise but are struggling to join others' games or create their own until they are confident in doing this independently. Suggest scripts that children can use themselves. Provide physical play access cards (see our online content!) for children to use.
Make game rules visible	Many children, not just those with a communication condition, find it hard to clearly articulate the rules of games. Also, verbal information disappears and can be forgotten. Use physical cards (like our playing cards!) to make game rules visible.
Create clubs for children with similar experiences to socialise	Make lunchtime or after-school clubs for children with communication conditions to join if they want to, where they can get to know one another, find common interests, and build friendships.

DOI: 10.4324/9781003332473-4

31

Get to know Zedie, Zoola, and friends

Zedie

"I like exploring rock pools and volleyball. I don't like heights or being late for things".

Zoola

"I like big days out, whistling, and dancing. I don't like ghosts or thunder and lightning".

Mishposh

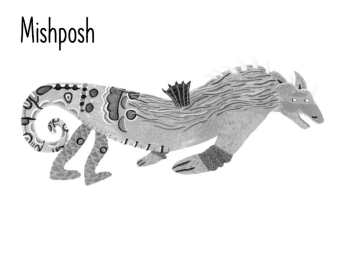

"I like music and swimming fast. I don't like spending a long time working something out".

Zeel

"I like being outdoors, looking after others, and making jams. I don't like crowded places".

Demshoo

"I like walks with friends, writing poems, and listening to trees. I don't like running or being the centre of attention".

Tibul

"I like getting muddy, talking, and taking photos. I don't like being hungry or being quiet in the cinema".

Miply

"I like windy weather, collecting rubbish on the beach, and solving problems. I don't like reading fiction books".

Wonpeel

"I like swimming and making things. I don't like itchy jumpers or sitting still for too long".

Limtop

"I like surfing and going to food markets where there are nice smells. I don't like the dark, so I always carry a torch".

Alya

"I like watching others, long journeys, and making dens. I don't like pickled onions or getting splinters".

Hishkit

"I like going to the theatre and having long conversations. I don't like dirt or tinned vegetables".

Kippo

"I like fizzy drinks, dancing, and beatboxing. I don't like long bus rides or waiting in queues".

Nipteef

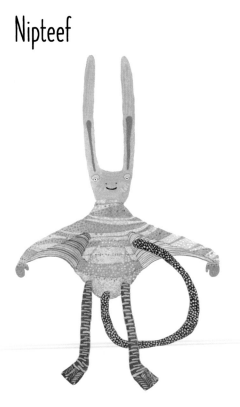

"I like asking questions, telling jokes, and tickling others. I don't like museums or sticking to the rules".

Pibbon

"I like the earliest part of the morning and parties. I don't like packed lunches or being alone".

Glorms

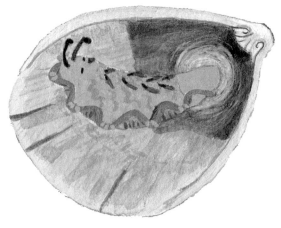

"We like finding warm places to sleep inside our shells. We don't like to be woken suddenly by loud noises".

The Alans

"We like having our hair cut and blow dried by Zeel. We don't like standing outside in the rain".

DOI: 10.4324/9781003332473-5

Using *Zedie & Zoola's Playful Universe*

A guide to using the playing cards

Step 1: Read the story *Zedie & Zoola Light Up the Night*

Find out about Zedie, Zoola, and all the other characters!

Step 2: Choose a card

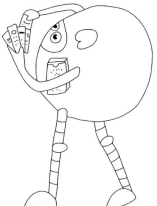

Pick one of the cards that you like the look of.

Step 3: Find a friend to play with

See who else wants to play.
What does the card say?
Read it together.

Step 4: Have fun!

Step 5: Swap the card when you're ready

When you want to play something different, choose a new card.

Step 6: After school, use your log-book

If you want to, you can use your log-book when you get home. Who did you play with today? What did you play? Write it down!

Top tip: You might like to laminate the cards, hole-punch them, and put them on a lanyard.

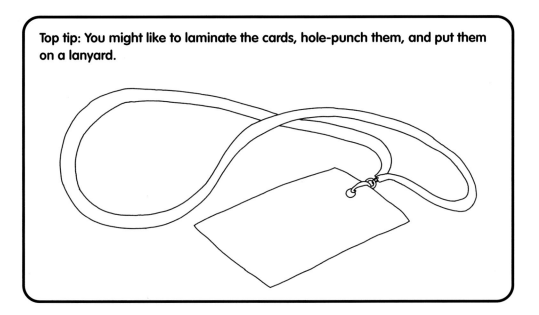

A note on age:

These cards have been designed with children aged 6+ in mind.

Someone who can read should help children who cannot read or children who find reading a challenge to become familiar with the game instructions.

This could be a friend, an older sibling, or a grownup.

Card symbols:

The key words on each card have their own picture symbol.
Lots of us find it helpful to use pictures to take in information.
These symbols are there to help us follow the game instructions.

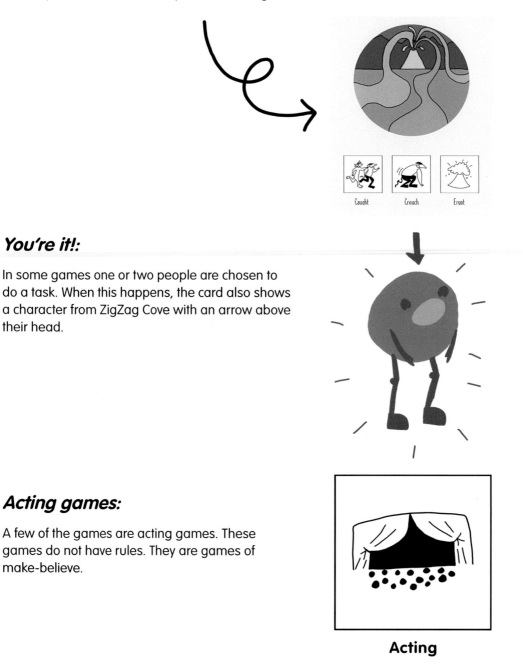

Caught   Crouch   Erupt

You're it!:

In some games one or two people are chosen to
do a task. When this happens, the card also shows
a character from ZigZag Cove with an arrow above
their head.

Acting games:

A few of the games are acting games. These
games do not have rules. They are games of
make-believe.

Acting

Itinerary of materials available online

You have access to premium online content. A number of these materials are also printed on the following pages, ready for photocopying.*

Playing card duplicates

- *In case any cards go missing, you can print new cards.*
- **Log-book**
- *Printable booklets for children to record their favourite games.*
- **Colouring sheets***
- *An alternative activity for when children prefer a break from the playground.*
- **Wall poster**
- *A poster of all the characters from* Zedie & Zoola Light Up the Night.
- **Sign board for the playground***
- *Print this board for display in the playground. Pointing to images and symbols is another way for us to get our message across.*
- **Play access cards***
- *Print and laminate these cards. Children can choose to use them to help them participate in games on the playground.*

For schools:

- **Lesson plan* and presentation**
- *Read the story* Zedie & Zoola Light Up the Night *aloud and use the PowerPoint presentation. Introduce the concept of neurodiversity to the class.*
- **Sign-out form***
- *Use to keep track of who's used the cards last.*

Tips for using *Zedie & Zoola's Playful Universe* at school:

To support everyone to understand the story

You might like to let children take the story home with them on a library system. Some children might like more time to process the storyline.

To share the Playful Universe cards fairly

Make the cards available at breaktime or lunchtime. Put them in a place where everyone in the class has access to them. Classrooms can take turns to pass the card pack around.

Tips for families:

Some of the games are two-player, others are for groups of more than two people.

Bring *Zedie & Zoola's Playful Universe* to your child's school or after-school clubs. Encourage the adults there to read the guidebook. Your child could then play the games with more than two friends in those environments.

You could also bring the game cards to friends' houses.

Log-book

Lesson presentation

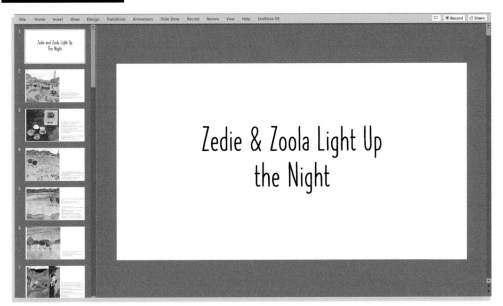

Wall poster

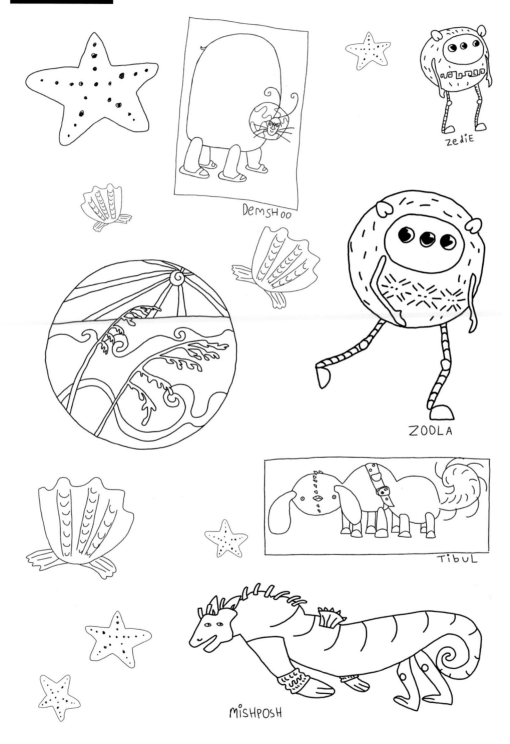

zediE

DemsHoo

ZOOLa

TibuL

MiSHPOSH

zedie

kippo

DEMSHOO

ALYA

WONPeel

MiPLY

GLORM

ZeeL

Limtop

HiSHKit

Nipteef

Pibbon

Sign

board

PLAY ACCESS CARDS

Available to print and laminate, for playtime use

Can you show
me how to play?

Can you tell me
the rules to the
game?

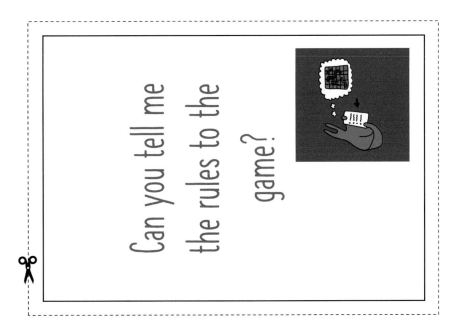

Time out

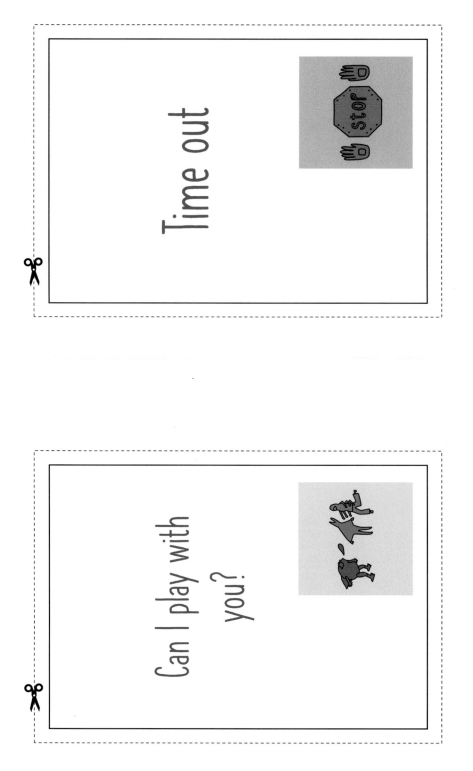

Can I play with you?

Copyright material from Lloyd-Esenkaya (2023), *Zedie & Zoola's Playful Universe*, Routledge

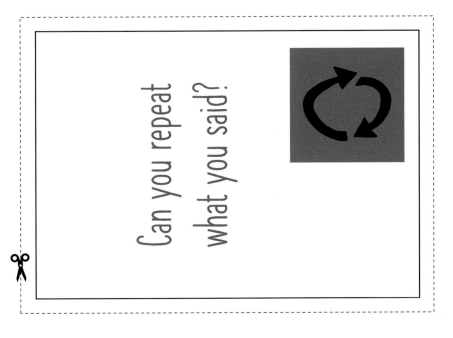

Can you repeat what you said?

Lesson plan

Building awareness of communication and communication conditions
Circle time ideas

Note: Speech, language, and communication needs are common. Developmental Language Disorder (DLD) alone is estimated to affect, on average, 2 in 30 children. This topic could be sensitive for some pupils in your class.

Lesson objectives

✓ Recognise that we are all different

✓ Understand what communication is

✓ Know how to help each other to join in at playtime

✓ Learn how to ask for help to communicate

Equipment you will need:

–A projector

–The presentation accompanying this lesson plan

–A flip chart or whiteboard

–All pupils to have a pen and a piece of paper or, ideally, a whiteboard

–Sticky notes

1. Open the lesson by helping pupils to understand that every person is different and unique

You could use the following activities:

- Ask the children to put up their hand if.... (they have brown hair, they like dancing, they don't like butter, etc)
  Who else in the room has their hand up?
  To ensure everyone can join in, use visuals. Write the words on the board as you go, with a tick or a cross, and allow plenty of time to respond.

- Ask the children to talk with the person sat next to them:
  Tell your partner something you are good at.
  Tell your partner something you find tricky/difficult.
  Encourage children to write this down or draw it (using paper or whiteboards).
  After each discussion ask if anyone wants to share.

2. Using a projector, present the story:
Zedie and Zoola Light Up the Night

Read the story aloud as you go through the PowerPoint presentation.

3. Circle time discussion of *Zedie and Zoola Light Up the Night.*

Establish your pupils' understanding of the story. You might want to use the following questions to lead this discussion:

What was the problem at ZigZag Cove?	What did Zedie find difficult to do?
What were Zedie and Zoola looking for, and why?	How might Zedie have felt when Mishposh left before Zedie finished talking?
Why was Zedie chosen for the task?	How might Zedie have felt when Tibul misunderstood what Zedie was trying to say?

To ensure everyone can join in, encourage children to write or draw their ideas on their whiteboards and hold these up. When a pupil shares an answer, write this on the board at the front of the class.

4. Activity to help pupils to understand what communication is

Show slide number 29 in the PowerPoint presentation to help explain to the class what communication is. You may wish to use this script:

"Communication is when we share information with other people. There are lots of ways we do this. We can share information by speaking and listening. We can use pictures. We can use our bodies to help describe things. And we can use sign language."

5. Share the benefits of helping others to join in at playtime

Help the pupils to realise that there are gains to be had when we take the time to include people. Show slide number 30 in the PowerPoint presentation and read aloud the description of Zedie. You may wish to link this to specific examples pupils gave of their own strengths/things they like from the start of the lesson.

Help the class to see that if the other characters hadn't taken the time to communicate with Zedie, they would never have got to know what Zedie was really like as a person.

6. Supporting pupils to help themselves and each other

Establish your pupils' understanding of the ways the characters helped Zedie to communicate. You might want to use the following questions to lead this discussion:

Do you remember any characters in the story who helped Zedie to share their message?	Do you remember what *tool* Zedie was given to make it easier to share their message? (the whiteboard)
What did Demshoo do when Tibul misunderstood what Zedie was trying to say?	What did Hishkit help Zedie to do?

To ensure everyone can join in, encourage children to write or draw their ideas on their whiteboards and hold these up. When a pupil shares an answer, write this on the board at the front of the class.

Show slide number 32 in the PowerPoint presentation to help the pupils to think about ways to make communication easier.

Ask the class: "Can you think of anything else that Zedie would find helpful?"

Ask the class to imagine that Zedie went to their school and was in their class. "What sorts of things might Zedie find tricky when it's playtime?"

It's possible that these discussions might help children with communication conditions to bring up ideas for ways to help them, on the playground or in the classroom. Keep a note of these ideas to support school staff to meet these children's participation needs.

Give all pupils 2 sticky notes.

Ask pupils to write down one thing they could do if they are find it hard to get their message across, or to know what others are saying.

Ask pupils to write down one thing they could do if they see someone having a hard time joining in at playtime.

Ask pupils to add their sticky notes to the board.

Optional follow-up activities

You may wish to:

7. Explain to the class how to use the game cards
Use Chapter 4 of the guidebook for guidance.

8. Ask the pupils to make their own log-books, using the print-outs, and fill in their profiles
Pupils could keep their log-book in their drawers/book bags at school, to add to at their leisure.

9. Print and laminate the play access cards, and explain to the class how to use them
It's hard for some of us to find the words to ask others to play. Children can choose to use the play access cards to help them participate in games on the playground.

10. Explain to the class how to use the sign-out sheet to keep track of who's used the cards last
Print the sheet and keep it somewhere accessible.

Sign-out form

Who played with the cards today?

Today's date	Name	Class	Played with cards today? (tick)	Brought cards back? (tick)	Card number(s)

References

1. Bercow, J. *Bercow: Ten Years On. Royal College of Speech and Language Therapists* https://www.bercow10yearson.com/wp-content/uploads/2018/04/Bercow-Ten-Years-On-Summary-Report-.pdf (2018).
2. Lane, H., Harding, S. & Wren, Y. A systematic review of early speech interventions for children with cleft palate. *Int. J. Lang. Commun. Disord.* **57**, 226–245 (2022).
3. Kuehn, D. P. & Moller, K. T. The state of the art: Speech and language issues in the cleft palate population. *Cleft Palate-Craniofacial J.* **37**, 348 (2000).
4. Cavalheiro, M. G., Lamônica, D. A. C., de Vasconsellos Hage, S. R. & Maximino, L. P. Child development skills and language in toddlers with cleft lip and palate. *Int. J. Pediatr. Otorhinolaryngol.* **116**, 18–21 (2019).
5. Chapman, R. S. & Hesketh, L. J. Language, cognition, and short-term memory in individuals with Down syndrome. *Downs. Syndr. Res. Pract.* **7**, 1–7 (2001).
6. Salikhova, K. & Salikhova, S. Speech disorders in children with down syndrome. *Cogent Med.* **6**, 38–41 (2019).
7. Langdon Down Museum of Learning Disability. Learning disability in the UK population. https://langdondownmuseum.org.uk/learning-disability/learning-disability-in-the-uk-population/.
8. Thapar, A. & Rutter, M. Genetic advances in autism. *J. Autism Dev. Disord.* **51**, 4321–4332 (2021).
9. Crompton, C. J., Ropar, D., Vans-Williams, C. V. M., Flynn, E. G. & Fletcher-Watson, S. Autistic peer to peer information transfer is highly effective. *Autism* **24**, 1–9 (2020) doi:10.31219/OSF.IO/J4KNX.
10. Sturrock, A., Chilton, H., Foy, K., Freed, J. & Adams, C. In their own words: The impact of subtle language and communication difficulties as described by autistic girls and boys without intellectual disability. *Autism.* **26** (2021) doi:10.1177/13623613211002047.
11. Donato, C., Spencer, E. & Arthur-Kelly, M. A critical synthesis of barriers and facilitators to the use of AAC by children with autism spectrum disorder and their communication partners. *AAC Augment. Altern. Commun.* **34**, 242–253 (2018).
12. Law, J. *et al. Early Language Development: Needs, provision, and intervention for preschool children from socio-economically disadvantaged backgrounds.* https://educationendowmentfoundation.org.uk/public/files/Law_et_al_Early_Language_Development_final.pdf (2017).
13. Bowyer-Crane, C. *et al. The impact of Covid-19 on School Starters: Interim briefing 1 Parent and school concerns about children starting school.* Education Endowment Foundation (2021).
14. Bowyer-Crane, C. *et al. Research Briefing – Early years settings and the COVID-19 Pandemic.* National Insitute of Economic and Social Research (2020).

References

15. Viola, T. W. & Nunes, M. L. Social and environmental effects of the COVID-19 pandemic on children. *J. Pediatr. (Rio. J).* **98**, 4–12 (2022).
16. Charney, S. A., Camarata, S. M. & Chern, A. Potential impact of the COVID-19 pandemic on communication and language skills in children. *Otolaryngol. – Head Neck Surg. (United States)* **165**, 1–2 (2021).
17. Fricke, S., Bowyer-Crane, C., Haley, A. J., Hulme, C. & Snowling, M. J. Efficacy of language intervention in the early years. *J. Child Psychol. Psychiatry Allied Discip.* **54**, 280–290 (2013).
18. Rose, S. C., Weldy, D. L., Zhukivska, S. & Pommering, T. L. Acquired stuttering after pediatric concussion. *Acta Neurol. Belg.* **2–3** (2021) doi:10.1007/s13760-021-01653-x.
19. Stockbridge, M. D. *et al.* Language profiles in children with concussion. *Brain Inj.* **34**, 567–574 (2020).
20. Kozin, E. D., Knoll, R. M. & Bhattacharyya, N. Association of Pediatric Hearing Loss and Head Injury in a population-based study. *Otolaryngol. – Head Neck Surg. (United States)* **165**, 455–457 (2021).
21. Cermak, C. A. *et al.* Cognitive communication impairments in children with traumatic brain injury: A scoping review. *J. Head Trauma Rehabil.* **34**, E13–E20 (2019).
22. Caplan, R. *et al.* Social communication in children with epilepsy. *J. Child Psychol. Psychiatry Allied Discip.* **43**, 245–253 (2002).
23. Völkl-Kernstock, S., Bauch-Prater, S., Ponocny-Seliger, E. & Feucht, M. Speech and school performance in children with benign partial epilepsy with centro-temporal spikes (BCECTS). *Seizure* **18**, 320–326 (2009).
24. Baumer, F. M., Cardon, A. L. & Porter, B. E. Language dysfunction in pediatric epilepsy. *J. Paediatr.* **194**, 13–21 (2018).
25. Peterson, R. K. *et al.* Characterizing language outcomes following childhood basal ganglia stroke. *Appl. Neuropsychol. Child* **10**, 14–25 (2021).
26. Greenham, M. *et al.* Social functioning following pediatric stroke: Contribution of neurobehavioral impairment. *Dev. Neuropsychol.* **43**, 312–328 (2018).
27. Westmacott, R., Askalan, R., Macgregor, D., Anderson, P. & Deveber, G. Cognitive outcome following unilateral arterial ischaemic stroke in childhood: Effects of age at stroke and lesion location. *Dev. Med. Child Neurol.* **52**, 386–393 (2010).
28. Buckeridge, K., Clarke, C. & Sellers, D. Adolescents' experiences of communication following acquired brain injury. *Int. J. Lang. Commun. Disord.* **55**, 97–109 (2020).
29. RCSLT. Paediatric stroke & childhood brain injury: A patient and therapist perspective. https://podcasts.apple.com/gb/podcast/paediatric-stroke-childhood-brain-injury-patient-therapist/id1523073475?i=1000529443822.
30. Meningitis Research Foundation. Speech, language and communication difficulties after acquired brain injury. https://www.meningitis.org/getmedia

/7b5e6bb0-3e80-4ed4-887b-91e220ad5162/Speech,-language-and
-communication-difficulties-after-acquired-brain-injury-August-2017.

31. Anderson, V., Anderson, P., Grimwood, K. & Nolan, T. Cognitive and executive function 12 years after childhood bacterial meningitis: Effect of acute neurologic complications and age of onset. *J. Pediatr. Psychol.* **29**, 67–81 (2004).

32. Kutz, J. W., Simon, L. M., Chennupati, S. K., Giannoni, C. M. & Manolidis, S. Clinical predictors for hearing loss in children with bacterial meningitis. *Arch. Otolaryngol. Neck Surg.* **132**, 941–945 (2006).

33. Malarbi, S., Abu-Rayya, H. M., Muscara, F. & Stargatt, R. Neuropsychological functioning of childhood trauma and post-traumatic stress disorder: A meta-analysis. *Neurosci. Biobehav. Rev.* **72**, 68–86 (2017).

34. Palazón-Carrión, E. & Sala-Roca, J. Communication and language in abused and institutionalized minors. A scoping review. *Child. Youth Serv. Rev.* **112**, (2020).

35. Clegg, J., Crawford, E., Spencer, S. & Matthews, D. Developmental Language Disorder (DLD) in young people leaving care in England: A study profiling the language, literacy and communication abilities of young people transitioning from care to independence. *Int. J. Environ. Res. Public Health* **18**, (2021).

36. Maguire, D., McCormack, D., Downes, C., Teggart, T. & Fosker, T. The impact of care-related factors on the language and communication needs of looked after and adopted children/young people. *Dev. Child Welf.* **3**, 235–255 (2021).

37. Norbury, C. F. Developmental Language Disorder: The most common childhood condition you've never heard of. *The Guardian* (2017).

38. Etchell, A. C., Civier, O., Ballard, K. J. & Sowman, P. F. A systematic literature review of neuroimaging research on developmental stuttering between 1995 and 2016. *J. Fluency Disord.* **55**, 6–45 (2018).

39. BBC Three. Things not to say to someone who stammers. *YouTube* https://www.youtube.com/watch?v=xlDi0bMNV6g (2017).

40. Bishop, D. V. M., Snowling, M. J., Thompson, P. L., Greenhalgh, P. & the CATALISE-2 consortium. Phase 2 of CATALISE: A multinational and multidisciplinary Delphi consensus study of problems with language development: Terminology. *J. Child Psychol. Psychiatry Allied Discip.* **58**, 1068–1080 (2017).

41. Norbury, C. F. *et al.* The impact of nonverbal ability on prevalence and clinical presentation of language disorder: Evidence from a population study. *J. Child Psychol. Psychiatry Allied Discip.* **57**, 1247–1257 (2016).

42. Bishop, D. V. M. & Hayiou-Thomas, M. E. Heritability of specific language impairment depends on diagnostic criteria. *Genes, Brain Behav.* **7**, 365–372 (2008).

43. Ullman, M. T., Earle, F. S., Walenski, M. & Janacsek, K. The neurocognition of developmental disorders of language. *Annu. Rev. Psychol.* **71**, 389–417 (2020).

44. Krishnan, S., Watkins, K. E. & Bishop, D. V. M. Neurobiological basis of language learning difficulties. *Trends Cogn. Sci.* **20**, 701–714 (2016).

References

45. RADLD. Lily Farrington's amazing developmental language disorder animation. *YouTube* https://www.youtube.com/watch?v=rwOfkj0dj_0 (2019).

46. RADLD. Life as an adult with Developmental Language Disorder (DLD). *YouTube* https://www.youtube.com/watch?v=bgSgvvPX-EY (2020).

47. Developmental Language Disorder. *Someone Like Me* https://www.rte.ie/radio/podcasts/22062492-developmental-language-disorder/ (2022).

48. Gallagher, A. L., Murphy, C., Conway, P. F. & Perry, A. Engaging multiple stakeholders to improve speech and language therapy services in schools: An appreciative inquiry-based study. *BMC Health Serv. Res.* **19**, 1–17 (2019).

49. Lester, S. & Russell, W. *Children's Right to Play. The SAGE Handbook of Play and Learning in Early Childhood.* Sage (2014). doi:10.4135/9781473907850.n25.

50. Play Wales. Play types. https://issuu.com/playwales/docs/play_types?e=5305098/53885121.

51. Burn, A. & Richards, C. *Children's Games in the New Media Age. Childlore, Media and the Playground.* Routledge (2014).

52. Gray, C. *et al.* What is the relationship between outdoor time and physical activity, sedentary behaviour, and physical fitness in children? A systematic review. *Int. J. Environ. Res. Public Health* **12**, 6455–6474 (2015).

53. Nijhof, S. L. *et al.* Healthy play, better coping: The importance of play for the development of children in health and disease. *Neurosci. Biobehav. Rev.* **95**, 421–429 (2018).

54. Kinoshita, I. & Woolley, H. Children's play environment after a disaster: The great East Japan earthquake. *Children* **2**, 39–62 (2015).

55. Fearn, M. & Howard, J. Play as a resource for children facing adversity: An exploration of indicative case studies. *Child. Soc.* **26**, 456–468 (2012).

56. Rao, Z., Gibson, J. & Nicholl, B. Features of social play in 8- to 11-year-olds in China: Exploring children's own perspectives. *Beijing Int. Rev. Educ.* **2**, 276–294 (2020).

57. Howard, J., Miles, G. E., Rees-Davies, L. & Bertenshaw, E. J. Play in middle childhood: Everyday play behaviour and Associated Emotions. *Child. Soc.* **31**, 378–389 (2017).

58. Milic, M. I., Carl, T. & Rapee, R. M. Similarities and differences between young children with selective mutism and social anxiety disorder. *Behav. Res. Ther.* **133**, 103696 (2020).

59. Barr, J., McLeod, S. & Daniel, G. Siblings of children with speech impairment: Cavalry on the hill. *Lang. Speech. Hear. Serv. Sch.* **39**, 21–32 (2008).

60. Lloyd-Esenkaya, V., Russell, A. J. & St Clair, M. C. What are the peer interaction strengths and difficulties in children with developmental language disorder? A systematic review. *Int. J. Environ. Res. Public Health* **17**, (2020).

61. Lloyd-Esenkaya, V., Forrest, C. L., Jordan, A., Russell, A. J. & Clair, M. C. S. What is the nature of peer interactions in children with language disorders ? A qualitative study of parent and practitioner views. *Autism Dev. Lan.* **6**, 1–17 (2021).

62. Jensen de López, K. M. *et al.* "So, I told him to look for friends!" Barriers and protecting factors that may facilitate inclusion for children with Language Disorder in everyday social settings: Cross-cultural qualitative interviews with parents. *Res. Dev. Disabil.* **115**, (2021).

63. Forrest, C. L., Gibson, J. L., Halligan, S. L. & St Clair, M. C. A longitudinal analysis of early language difficulty and peer problems on later emotional difficulties in adolescence: Evidence from the Millennium Cohort Study. *Autism Dev. Lang. Impair.* **3**, 1–15 (2018).

64. Blood, G. W. & Blood, I. M. Long-term consequences of childhood bullying in adults who stutter: Social anxiety, fear of negative evaluation, self-esteem, and satisfaction with life. *J. Fluency Disord.* **50**, 72–84 (2016).

65. Edmondson, S. & Howe, J. Exploring the social inclusion of deaf young people in mainstream schools, using their lived experience. *Educ. Psychol. Pract.* **35**, 216–228 (2019).

66. Van den Bedem, N. P., Dockrell, J. E., Van Alphen, P. M., Kalicharan, S. V & Rieffe, C. Victimization, bullying, and emotional competence: Longitudinal associations in (pre)adolescents with and without Developmental Language Disorder. *J. Speech Lang Hear Res.* **61**, 2021–2044 (2018) doi:10.1044/2018_JSLHR-L-17-0429.

67. Bouldin, E. *et al.* Bullying and children who are deaf or hard-of-hearing: A scoping review. *Laryngoscope* **131**, 1884–1892 (2021).

68. MultiMind. *Multilingualism & Developmental Language Disorder.* https://www.multilingualmind.eu/_files/ugd/850b63_841a36a7cd194a38974d31d21cd27f0c.pdf (2021).

69. Novogrodsky, R. & Meir, N. Multilingual children with special needs in early education. In *Handbook of Early Language Education*, edited by M. Schwartz. Springer, 1–29 (2020) doi:10.1007/978-3-030-47073-9_18-1.

70. Müller, L. M., Howard, K., Wilson, E., Gibson, J. & Katsos, N. Bilingualism in the family and child well-being: A scoping review. *Int. J. Biling.* **24**, 1049–1070 (2020).

Recommended reading

I would recommend the following resources to anyone keen to know more about the topics raised in this book:

- Fletcher-Watson, S. (2021). *Neurodiversity: What is it and how can we apply it?* https://www.youtube.com/watch?v=gdTFS7P810U&t=1954s, accessed 28 April 21.
- Wong, A. (ed.). (2020). *Disability Visibility: First-person Stories from the Twenty-first Century.* New York: Vintage.
- Runswick-Cole, K., Curran, T. & Liddiard, K. (eds.). (2018). *The Palgrave Handbook of Disabled Children's Childhood Studies* (pp. 425–442). London: Palgrave Macmillan.

References

- Battye, A. (2017). *Who's Afraid of AAC? The UK Guide to Augmentative and Alternative Communication*. Abingdon, UK: Routledge.
- The Royal College of Speech and Language Therapist's (RCSLT) factsheets https://www.rcslt.org/speech-and-language-therapy/#section-8
- I CAN, a children's communication charity https://ican.org.uk/
- Afasic, a charity for young people with Speech, Language, and Communication Needs, and their families https://www.afasic.org.uk/
- Stamma, a charity for stammering https://stamma.org/
- Constantino, C., Campbell, P. & Simpson, S. (2022). Stuttering and the social model. *Journal of Communication Disorders*, https://doi.org/10.1016/j.jcomdis.2022.106200
- Campbell, P. (2019). *Stammering Pride and Prejudice*. J & R Press Limited.
- RADLD, a charity for Developmental Language Disorder (DLD) https://radld.org/
- Sowerbutts, A. & Finer, A. (2019). *DLD and Me: Supporting Children and Young People with Developmental Language Disorder*. Abingdon, UK: Routledge.
- Engage with DLD, an academic organisation for research into Developmental Language Disorder https://www.engage-dld.com/
- National Deaf Children's Society, a charity for deaf children and their families https://www.ndcs.org.uk/
- Positive about Down syndrome, a charity by and for families of children with Down syndrome https://positiveaboutdownsyndrome.co.uk/
- Selective Mutism Association (SMA), an organisation for selective mutism https://www.selectivemutism.org/
- National Autistic Society, an organisation for autism https://www.autism.org.uk/
- Davis, R., & Crompton, C. J. (2021). What do new findings about social interaction in autistic adults mean for neurodevelopmental research? *Perspectives on Psychological Science*, https://doi.org/10.1177/1745691620958010
- Play Wales, a charity for children's right to play in Wales https://www.playwales.org.uk/eng/
- Play England, a charity for children's right to play in England https://www.playengland.org.uk/what-we-do
- Play in Education Development and Learning (PEDAL), an academic organisation for research into play https://www.pedalhub.org.uk/our-research
- Tiny Happy People, a BBC resource hub to support families with their child's communication skills https://www.bbc.co.uk/tiny-happy-people

Index

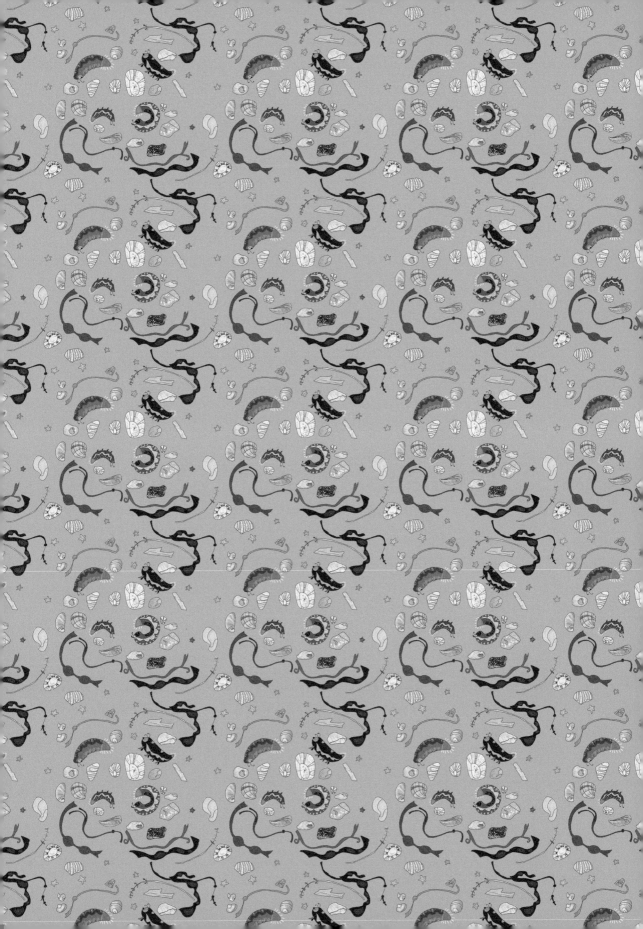

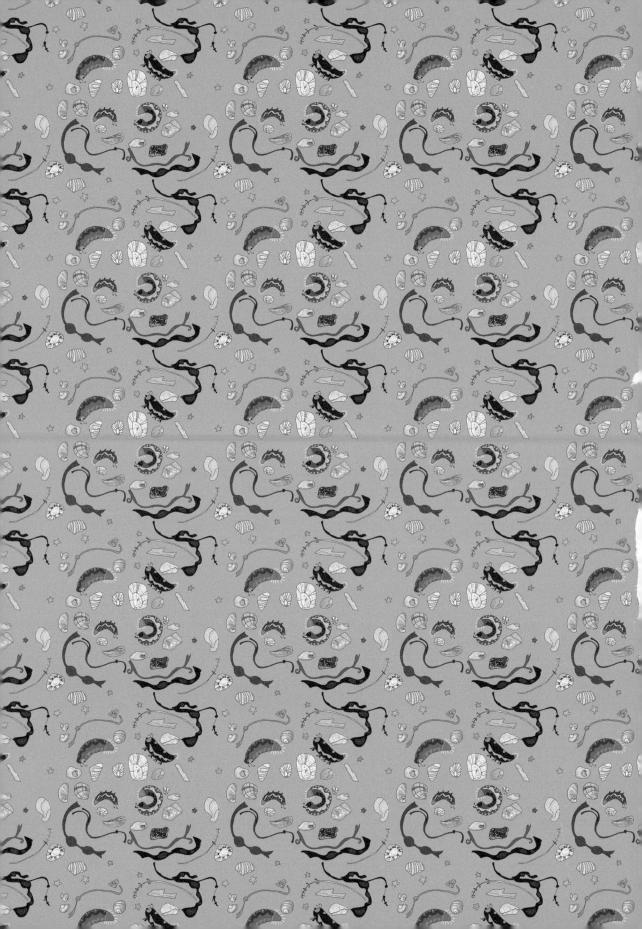